Dedicated to Tina,
My Muse, My Inspiration,
My Love.
Always with you
Forever, yours
Yours N V x

To Sarah, Louisa & Haych
Thank you for reminding me Of my worth.

CONTENTS

MEET MY DEMON.

My demon doesn't have a corporeal form.
But it's as real to me as you are.
It's with me, always.
It brings back not so new thoughts/feelings that I had for you.
That I thought I had buried long ago
When I decided that no good would come of them.
The situation hasn't changed, if anything it is even less possible now than it was back then when I could have, possibly, done something about it.

The longing. The ache in my chest that won't leave until I see you again.
The infinitesimal time we are together where nothing matters but the one I long for. Being in your presence is enough to quieten the demon for a while.

But as soon as I leave, the dark creeps back in, swallowing me whole, welcoming me back from my hiatus. Pulling me deeper than I've ever been before. It's hands encompassing my very being like a small child being welcomed into the world by its eager parents.

Each time I leave you it becomes harder and harder not to listen to the purr of the demon. Enticing me to do something stupid.
It's voice is like a consistent dripping tap that never stops, constantly putting me down, forever echoing my deepest darkest desires and fears.

The demon cherishes his time with me.
Grows stronger the longer I'm with it.
Increases its hold around my mind.
Caresses my thoughts with images of ending it all, how peaceful

I would be if I would just take the pills, slip the knife in a little deeper, jump off the bridge I walked past the other day. Anything to get me in its clutches for real.

For those that commit suicide don't go to heaven.

So, ignore the demon I must.
To keep the promise I made to you.
No matter how much I would love to give in.
For my love for you is greater than my need to not be here right now.
There may come a time when that isn't the case, and that day I wait for, quietly and reverently, for I know it WILL come. Eventually.
The day when you see the real me.
When the demon manages to reveal my true face to you.
I'm sure you've seen it glistening in my eye, a twinkle, there one moment gone the next.
But you dismiss it, as a trick of the light.
You dismiss the thought as ridiculous and stupid.
It does make you take a step back, however.
An unconscious act when you sense danger near.
But when you look again, I've regained control, the immediate danger has passed so you forget you saw it.

Until it reappears again.
This time for longer. The fear thick in your throat as you see in my eyes what you have secretly feared. That I have given in to my demon. Let it take control. You no longer see me as you used to, but the real me
Raw
Unhinged
Broken
Evil.
Your own personal demon.

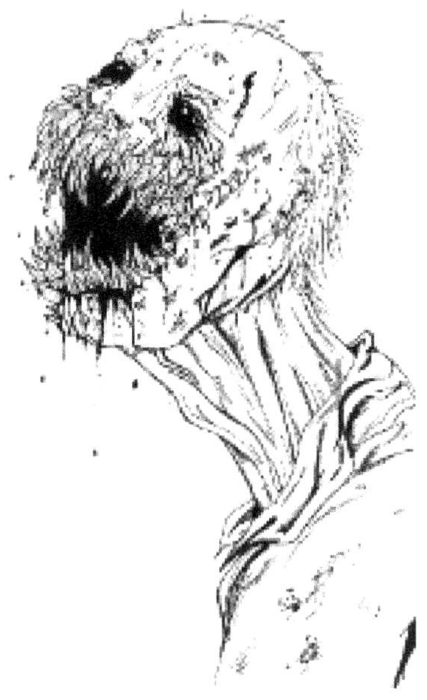

DEMON II

My demon consumed me over the weekend.
I thought there was nothing left of me. Just an empty shell.

But, thanks to an untimely, intervention, I'm still here.
So I've decided I'm going to fight it until my last breath, or until he no longer has the majority of the time in my head.
When he is nothing but a whisper on the wind, there but barely noticeable.

I need to look forward.
Concentrate on the good things.
Be more proactive.
Get my head straight.

I know there will be bad days.
Where his seductive tones will pull me back in again. But I need to resist, as best I can.
Not let him consume me again.

My family love me
My friends love me.
I don't know why they do, but they insist they do.
Although, when at my lowest point my family and friends just don't come into it.
I'm so deep into the blackness that I can't see the good/light things.
The blackness hides everyone and everything.

That's what it was like at the weekend.
Complete darkness.
Any light being blocked from my view.
The only thing that mattered to me was not being here anymore.
Getting away from the hurt. Hurting those that intervened. That

scuppered the plans.

I call my demon a he, but in truth he has many voices.
My mother.
My abuser.
My older sister.
Even my best friend has a voice, but it's distorted like it's not really them. Or maybe it is and I'm just not seeing their narrative clearly yet.
Me.
Each as loud as each other.
Sometimes they take it in turns.
Other times they're all shouting at the same time. Vying to be at the top. To be the one to break me.
Me. Nearly won this weekend. I think this one is the hardest to resist. But it is distractible.

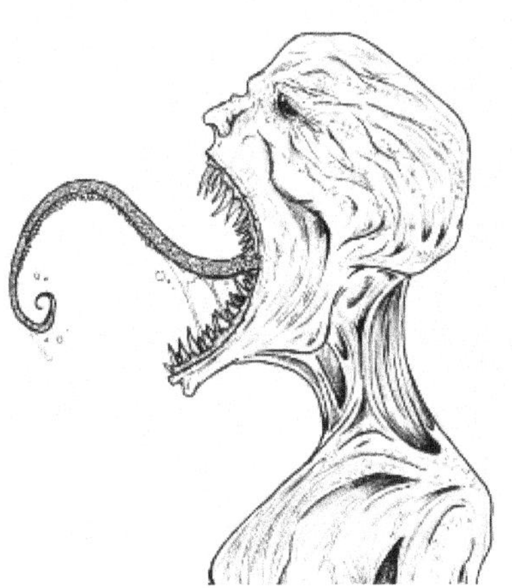

Having so many components it's hard to juggle, filter out the ones that don't mean as much harm as the others that are present.

I need to try and speak to each one individually - find out what they want or need, to give me peace from them.
Which ones mean to do me the most harm and figure out why.

I hope I'm strong enough.

BETRAYAL

I told you the truth
After more years than I care to admit
I told you the truth
And you baulked and left me there gasping
I told you that I loved you and now I'm more alone than ever.

I'm broken
Broken beyond belief
I'm broken
The pieces scattered far and wide.

There's nothing left to fix
There's nothing left to repair
There's nothing left.
Just me, and existential nothing.

I had nothing to offer, but myself
As shattered as I am.
I have nothing to entice you to leave your man.

So slip into the background I must
Again. Watching from afar.
Hiding my affections.
Like I have done for the last 15 years.

WAITING 1

I feel set adrift.
Floating away on the ocean.
With nothing to anchor me to this life.

Waiting. Waiting for someone, something to rescue me.
But there is no one.
Just me.
In my pit of despair.
My demon has taken control.
I don't want to fight it anymore.
I can't fight it anymore.

THOUGHTS

Thoughts.
Thoughts circling
Circling like crows.
Crows that hang around dead things.
Things like death circle
Circle constantly
Constantly like the days turn into months
Months of pain
Pain everywhere
Everywhere broken
Broken and shattered
Shattered like a mirror
Mirror shows the real me
Me, broken by overthinking.

YOU ARE

You are my anchor. You keep me from floating away.
You are my life jacket. You keep me from drowning.
You are my lighthouse, directing me home.
You are my northern star. You light the way when I'm in a dark place.
You are my compass, keeping me on the right track.
You are my hope, when I'm in despair.
You are all of the above and so much more.

Without you, I am lost and alone.
Without you, I have no direction.
Without you, I drown.
Without you, the darkness wins.
Without you, I am nothing.

Without me, you are fine.
Without me, you are free.
Without me, you can thrive.
Without me, you are happy.

I am worthless.
I am flawed.
I am broken.

FIGHT OR SINK

I've been set adrift, away from civilisation
I've been, barely, floating for months
I'm trying to decide whether to try to fight the waves to swim back to civilisation
Waste all of my energy, on what will turn out to be a useless endeavour, or
To let the darkness, from the water around me consume me, again.
Make me a part of it. Welcome me into its clutches, that it's been trying so hard to tempt me for ages.
Could I play a different hand?
Could I maybe convince the darkness that I was succumbing and then at the very last moment hit it where it hurts the most, and bring myself back into the light?
Is it worth it?

Do I fight against the waves that are pushing me further and further away from the light, until I am exhausted and unable to fight the darkness when it comes for me, for it will. It tasted what it was like to have me, even if only temporarily.
Do I stay drifting, hoping that another lost soul will team up with me, that we can somehow help each other back into the light?
Or do I let the darkness take me willingly? Let it end my suffering. Let it take me away from my shit existence?
I haven't decided which option to take yet, or even if I'm strong enough to choose one.

Maybe I'll just drift in this gulf for the rest of my life.
Being pulled down partially, only to have a hand pull me back and then leave me there gasping for air. Waiting for the cycle to repeat itself. Staying under for longer each time, until eventually

no hand can reach down far enough to retrieve me.

At which point I won't care and will welcome the end when it comes, like an old friend. Letting it embrace me, like a long lost lover.

Why did I fight so hard against it? This is where I've wanted to be. Enfolded in the embrace of death, as it finally welcomed me home.

DARKNESS

Darkness,
Darkness everywhere.
Which way is up?
Which way is down?
Where is the exit?
There.
A flash of light.
But it's gone as quick as it came.
I stand in what I believe to be the middle of a vast room.
Listening to the silence.
Feeling suffocated by the dark and silence.
Another flash of light ahead.
It lasts a little longer this time.
I take a few steps forward, towards where I think the light is.
I stop. Try to get my bearings.
But I can't see anything.
Another flash of light.
This time to my right.
I run towards it.
And almost make it before it disappears again.
I stop, my breathing harsh in my ears.
I wait.
And wait.
For the light to show itself again.

I turn on the spot.
Trying to make something, anything, out.
A vague outline, a glimpse of another.
But there is nothing and no one.
I am completely alone.
My breathing has settled back to its normal rhythm.

Again, silence.

I keep turning my head, searching out the light that had so tempted me earlier.

I think I hear a whisper, coming from ahead of me.
I cautiously take a step forwards, back the way I came. Trying to find who the voice belongs to.
"Come with me" it whispers. "I can stop it all" it promises.
I find myself smiling. Finally, A solution.
I walk faster and faster. Trying to find the voice.
I hesitate, a feeling of dread has just swept over me.
"Come, you're so close" is purred just ahead of me "reach out, take my hand" it insists.

I don't move.
I look around, and see the light again.
It's in the opposite direction.
I have a choice to make.
Run towards the light, which I may never get too, or take one more step towards whatever is offering me salvation.
Do I continue to keep chasing the light around this vast room?
Or do I give in? And be surrounded by darkness forever?

TEMPTATION

I sit, looking at the knife.

It's razor sharp edge glistening in the light when I move my head from side to side.

Mocking me. Knowing I don't want to use it.

Not for the purpose that has been rolling through my mind the last few hours.

But I am so close to the edge.

Just another step forward and the edge of the cliff would crumble, and I'd go along with the rocks into the sea below.

I don't have a safety harness to save me.

I don't have anything.

Just my will power. And it's wavering.

To be free from everything.

To not have to deal with it all anymore.

I sit clutching the plastic bag in my hands.

Preparing to stick it over my head.

To suffocate myself.

I can't do this anymore.

I don't want to be here anymore.

I want my pills back.

I chose that way as it was the least gruesome and I could look asleep and not dead to whoever found me.

There would be no blood or injuries, it would just look like I passed in my sleep, completely natural.

Only I would know the truth, the evidence long since gotten rid of.

WAITING 2

Sitting on the precipice
Waiting for, I don't know what.
A sign. An intervention.
Anything that tells me what to do next.

I feel like I've been here my whole life.
Frozen to this spot, waiting on someone or something to give me a
purpose.
To take control.

A few people have tried, but they have been unable to move me.
They stayed with me for a while, but in the end they moved on, left
me here, on the edge.
Alone. Scared. Angry. Frustrated. Sad. Despondent. Empty.

I sit and wait for the one that is willing to sit with me for as long
as it takes.

DESPAIR

I'm a bomb.
Primed and ready to go off.
The fuse has been lit, years ago.
The flame is getting closer and closer to the ignition point.
Leave. Get out. Before it's too late and I take you with me.

Im a bottom feeder.
Scavenging for the scraps of what's left of my life.
The pieces scattered far and wide.
I can't cover enough ground to retrieve them all.

I'm a lost soul
I have no direction.
Wandering around the abyss blindly.
Waiting for my time to come.

I'm a lost cause.
Give up. Walk away. Save yourself.
I'm too far gone, to resurrect from this hell.
Remember me as I was not as I am now.

Broken.
Fractured.
Splintered into a million pieces.

Fragmented.
Subdued.
Overwhelmed.
Damaged beyond repair.

There is no hope left for me.

REDEMPTION?

I'm hanging on the edge of a cliff.
Barely. My fingernails have gone, I've been hanging that long.

Someone approaches. I call out.
"Help, Please, Help!"
I hear a maniacal laugh, that gets louder the closer it gets.
The owner of the laugh looks over the edge to the ravine at the bottom. The gushing of the rushing river a monotonous hum, a bass to the tinkle of the strangers laughter.
They look me in the eyes, smile, and then stamp on my fingers.
I fall.
Backwards.
Towards my death.
Just before I reach the bottom, I smile.

Finally, finally, I've been freed from my hell.
You see the devil had cursed me to hang there until someone decided whether to help me up or to watch me fall.
A few people had tried to pull me up, but the devil had weighted my shoes, so nobody was strong enough. They never tried for long.
But I was never supposed to have been pulled up.
I was being punished, punished for everything I'd done. All the people that I'd hurt.

This stranger was the only one who knew what to do, what needed to be done.
To let me go.
To free me from my constraints.
To set me on my new path, to redemption.
Except as my body hit the water, the devil appeared before me.
"There is no redemption for you, only more hell" his voice rattled

around my skull, bouncing off the bone and reverberating in my ear. He clicked his fingers, and when I opened my eyes again I was still falling.

Falling into the mouth of a volcano.

Where I was to spend the rest of my afterlife burning.

Burning for my sins.

Burning for all eternity.

SHADOWS

I've always lived in the shadows.
Watching, observing, never interfering.

There have been a few occasions when a special person could see me.
Could interact with me.
Would bring me into their light for a time.
But, it always ended the same.
With me going back to my safe shadows.

Where no one can hurt me.
Where no one can find me.

The things I've seen observing the world around me from my vantage point would probably turn your hair white.
Drunken fumbles.
Arguments.
The birth of a first born.
The death of a loved one.
War & Peace, Famine and Natural Disasters.

I have emerged voluntarily myself on two occasions.
To talk to someone, who was on the brink of doing something they wouldn't be able to come back from.
The first, took hours, but they eventually thanked me and went on to live until an old age and were happy for the majority of that life.
The second, jumped.

Now I hide.
With my eyes closed.
The world is a cruel place.
And I no longer want to be a part of it.

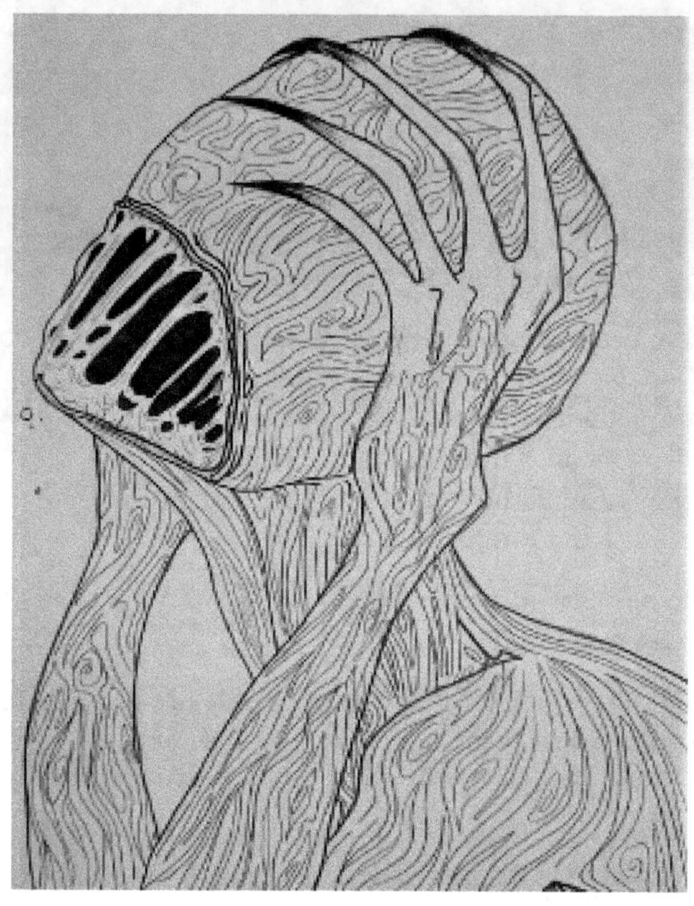

INTRUDER

Who am I?
I don't recognise myself anymore.
I'm quick to anger.
Abusive.
Violent.
Horrible.
Frustrated.

When I look in the mirror
I don't see myself anymore.
I see the sadness.
The broken pieces floating, waiting for me or someone else to grab them and put them back where they belong. But they are just an illusion.
I see the anger and frustration at not recognising the person staring back at me.

I want to harm the intruder that's using my body.
The intruder that makes me do and think things I don't want to do or think about.

Im in a constant battle.
Trying to take back control.
Fighting as hard as I can.
But the intruder is strong, and has almost taken full control.

The intruder has ruined my life.
My relationships.
My mind.

There is nothing left to salvage.

Maybe I should give in.
Let it take over completely.
Become the dormant, silent partner in this relationship.
A relationship I didn't consent to.

Fighting for my life, to make my voice heard everyday is so tiring.
I can feel I'm getting weaker by the day, hour, minute.
There will be nothing left of me soon.
I should just give in to the inevitable.

But I've never been a quitter.
I'll fight to the bitter end.
And if I lose, at least I'll know
I gave my all.

Or maybe this is who I am, really.
And I've already beaten the intruder.
They're the one that's faded into the background.
Stopped fighting the real me.
I subdued it months ago and I've been in complete control for the last few months.
And everything that's happened has been my own fault.
Self destructing
Ruining everything that ever meant anything to the old me.
And to explain it away, I blame 'the demon' or 'the intruder'

I don't know how we coincided together for so long when our goals and attitudes towards everything were polar opposites.

This was always going to end one way.
With an implosion, where neither of us wins.

Or maybe there's only ever been me.
And I'm responsible for everything that's happened.
I'm just a really shit human being.
Looking for ways to not blame myself, to try
and defend my actions.

Who am I?

A GOOD DAY

Today was a good day.
It's important to recognise a good day as well as the bad, especially when the good are few and far between.
Even the ok days should be acknowledged, for they are as important, as it shows nothing triggered you, you managed to keep your head. Pat yourself on the back on those days.
Treat yourself on the good days and contemplate, but ultimately LET GO of the bad ones.
Identify what made it bad, and think of a way you can improve the situation should it happen again.

Keep with it and soon the good days will far outweigh the bad.

Be grateful for the little things.
The people in your life.
The steps you've taken.

Go on, look over your shoulder.
Just look at how far you've come already.
There is still a way to go, and you may fall back a step or two.
But you HAVE to keep fighting.
Keep pushing.
Keep your head held high.

You can and will beat this.
And when you do you'll look back and you won't even be able to see what it was that troubled you so.
It'll be too far in the distance for you to see.
A small speck, amongst the dust motes that are always flying around, but you only see when the light shines on them just right.

That's what you aim for.
Then the sky's the limit.

You've got this.
Stay strong.
Have faith in yourself.

THE MIRROR

The mirror never lies.
When you look in the mirror
And all you see staring back at you
Is all of your faults, blemishes, scars, moles the hatred you have for yourself shining in your eyes.
It makes it very difficult to try and love yourself.
When you've seen yourself that way for so long, you automatically look away when a mirror is in view, because you can't stand the mocking indignant self loathing you know you'll see in your own eyes.

Friends try to tell you that what you see isn't true, that the scars show how strong you were to have gotten through.

But, the deep rooted belief that you aren't good enough, that you deserve every bad thing that comes your way.
That you don't deserve friends or anyone's time and care.
That everyone would be better off without you.
That nobody would notice if you disappeared off the face of the earth.
Is so hard to shake off.

It's difficult in the beginning to take their words as true. You brush it off with a snort or a thought of they're just saying that. They don't really care.

They can tell you every day that you are worthy, that you are cared for, that they love having you around.
But until you can banish your own belief there is no space to see what they see in you.

You need to try and cast off your self loathing beliefs, so that a new set of beliefs can take its place.

Beliefs that are kinder to you.
Allows you to see yourself, as if for the first time.
The help you've given to others.
Everything you've come through and you're still here, fighting, trying your best to piece yourself back together.
Parts may not fit anymore, not where they used to go, but you can grow and cultivate new parts that will fit in the empty space.
A kinder, more therapeutic piece.

Throw out the pieces that are crumbling even as you're watching.
Throw them out and never look back.
Fit the new pieces, let them shine and make you whole once more.

Believe in what others tell you about yourself.
They didn't need to make that comment, but they felt you needed to hear it.
Embrace it.
Squeeze it into your chest until it takes root in your heart and can spread the good around your body, diluting the bad/evil.

A time will come where you will be able to look into a mirror and smile at what you see, will purposefully walk up to the mirror and stand there and take in your radiant smile, your golden aura shimmering around you.

Then you'll know you've made it.
Then you'll know that you love yourself.

CLOSE.

I sit in my room, in silence.
Although it hasn't been silent for me, for months, not really.
The thoughts rolling in my mind. They are always there, reminding me, calling me out on my shit. Degrading me. Punishing me.

Tears begin to fall down my cheeks.
I don't even bother to wipe them away anymore.
I barely feel them as they travel down my cheeks, to drop down onto my shirt from my chin.

The pain, the guilt, the innocence taken consuming me. Again. And again.
I've learnt to cry in silence.
So nobody knows.
So nobody can console me.

The weight of it all crushing me.
Breaking me.
Until there's nothing of the old me left.
Just this empty shell that somehow manages to function, to go to work, talk to people, convince people that I'm doing okay.

It's only a matter of time until the carcass breaks too. Then there will be nothing holding the thoughts inside. They will be free to wreak havoc, free to destroy everything I used to hold dear.

And I'll be a passenger, watching but unable to stop any of it. Watching numbly as my own hands destroy my possessions. Watching as those same hands pick up the knife and bring it to my throat. I close my eyes, and whisper I'm ready.

But the fatal slice never comes.

The thoughts have given me control back.
I look around at the destruction surrounding me. And fall to my knees in despair.

So close that time, so fucking close.

FALLING

I've cried a thousand tears.
But still they keep falling.
Is it going to be like this for years?
I don't want to keep bawling.

I'm floating, aimlessly, with no direction as to where to go.
There is nothing tethering me anymore.
I'm just waiting, but I don't know what for.

I used to have complete control over my emotions.
Could stop crying in a second.
I hadn't shed a tear in years.
Monotony was the state of play.

I need to do that again.
Become the unfeeling robot I've been for the
last 6years.
At least then I could function.
Because, right now, I'm so so tired.
The thought of just giving in is so tempting.
I don't have the fight left to make it to the end.
I'll sleep now, and hope somehow
in that restful exercise the
answers to all my
questions will be answered

I AM WORTH IT

I am worth it.
People do care
It isn't going to be this bad forever.

Keep saying these to yourself, whenever the opposite thought pops, immediately say whichever counteracts it.
Eventually the negative one will disappear, not appear as often.

I am worth it.
People do care
It isn't going to be this bad forever.

Have faith in yourself. You are so worth it.
People absolutely do care. Just look around.
Keep chugging along, as long as you are still moving you can't be defeated.

I am worth it.
People do care
It isn't going to be this bad forever.

It's about time you did things for yourself, to appreciate what you do for others. Be selfish. Do something purely for you once in a while.
Friends tell you they care all the time. You get asked how you're doing every day. Listen to them. These people care about you.
Don't take their feelings as false, that isn't fair.
Yes, it's been pretty awful the last few months, but prior to that you were coping, even enjoyed life to a certain extent.
You will get back to that.

Baby steps. Baby steps.

I am worth it.

People do care
It isn't going to be this bad forever.

WELLNESS

That thought that just crossed your mind.
Yes, that one.
Let it go.

Procrastinating over something you can't control is a waste of your depleted energy reserves.

Try to focus on the things that you can control.

Self care.
Have a bath.
Light some scented candles.
Put on a face mask.
Put on some soothing music and relax.

Work.
You were chosen for the position you have, so your employer/ manager believes you can do it. If your workload has gotten too big for you to cope with - admit it. Nobody will think any differently of you for asking for assistance.
Try and bond with work colleagues, you spend more time at work than you do with family, so cultivate those relationships so that they enrich your life.

Family.
I know sometimes family can be part of the problem, but even so, they love you.
Try and arrange a meet up once a month.
Catch up on the latest goings on.
But only stay for as long as you are comfortable with. When you start to feel jittery, wind up the conversation and leave.

You are allowed to leave or remove yourself from any situation

you find yourself in.
You don't have to please anyone. Apart from yourself.

Had an invite to a party, but don't fancy attending? Then don't.
Read a book sat in your garden under the stars.
Don't want to do the laundry today? Then don't. Sit and watch an episode of your favourite television show.

Not everything needs doing NOW.
You're putting too much pressure on yourself.
Close your eyes. Take a deep breath and hold it for four seconds.
Then release it slowly.
Now open your eyes.
The first thing you focus on, do it. Whatever it is.

Treat yourself when you've managed to do something. Even if it's just getting out of bed and cleaning your teeth.
Some days that's all you'll be able to manage. And that's ok.

Go and make yourself your favourite soothing drink, and drink it in silence.
What can you hear? Birds twittering in the garden. Children playing a few doors away. Maybe cars rushing past your property?
Enjoy this moment of solitude.
Try to keep your mind clear.
Don't let the thoughts consume you.

You may now feel able to tackle the overflowing laundry basket, or the sink full of dishes that has been mocking you for the last three days.
If not - don't worry about it.
When you have more energy, you can do it then.

Just, take care of yourself, because no one else can do that for you.
Nobody knows you as well as you know yourself.

You've got this.

CROSSROADS

I find myself at a crossroads
And I don't know which way to go.

One will eventually lead back to you, but it won't be as it was
The other is a complete unknown.

Do I still want you as a part of my journey, the way I always
pictured it?
Do you still want me as part of your journey?
Or has too much passed between us?

The path without you looks to be overgrown with brambles and
thorns. There could be a rainbow at the end, but it's too far away to
see. Too dark as the sun is blocked out.

The path with you also has the brambles and thorns, but they've
been cut back so the way is slightly easier. Less cumbersome.
But just around the bend there could be another obstacle, a wall
we'd need to scale, a fire breathing dragon that we have to tame.

Do I want to face the perils of either journey without you? Can I?
Can you?
I do have others along for my journey now, for however long they
can stand to be battling with me.

I know if I was alone, I'd have lost my way and probably been burnt
to a crisp by now.
You have always been my moral compass. Directing me, even
when you didn't realise it.
Can I take the lead?
Can I take responsibility for my own future?
Can I do this without you?
Do I even have a choice?

CONFUSED

I'm confused.
Not for the first time
And I doubt it will be my last

You said you cared about me, like family
And then I get abandoned when things get rough
When I needed you most.

I was never your priority
You'd made that perfectly clear
And I was okay with the scraps that were left over
As I could make those scraps into what I needed.

I'm resourceful that way
But you didn't like it
When you found out
You didn't even want me having those
So you collected them up, And turned your back.

Now I'm here, alone and missing pieces of myself
As when you collected your parts
Some of mine got mixed in there too
They aren't vital parts but I feel their absence as keenly as you.

I try to grow and cultivate new pieces to overlay and make the holes stronger,
So that it is harder for the next person to get in so deep, to remove part of me.
There won't be anything of the original me left soon
So when you next see me, you won't recognise me.
You'll just walk past, a blank stare on your face as you carry on living your life, without me, carrying my extra pieces with you, unknowingly.

My pieces will recognise me, as everyone has their own frequency.
Ours used to match and make beautiful music, but not anymore.
It's more like a clash of a cymbal followed by emptiness as the noise travels outward.
Trying to find the other that compliments it so well.

But, my original stolen pieces don't fit anymore. The shapes have been changed through time and healing.
My frequency has changed ever so slightly, but it's enough that we now don't compliment the other rather we clash. Like thunder after the lightning. Disagreeing.

You can keep the pieces you have, I'm happy as I am.

HOLE OR WHOLE?

When you walked away
You left behind a chasm
So big and wide
Filling it seems impossible.

I'm pulling at the edges
Trying to make them stretch
I've ripped parts off
In my desperate attempt

I don't know if it will ever heal
Be the same again
Or whether a new someone
Will help me to overcome

I sit here with this ragged hole
Gaping in my chest
Wondering why you don't have the same
How are you still whole? And perfect?

I'll wander this world alone from now on
Searching for I don't know what
But on my quest, know this
I am moving on.

WORDS

Disturbed

Deadly

Demonic

Defensive

Evil

Explosive

Egotistical

Empty

Bitter

Bad

Banal

Brute

Ogreish

Oblivious

Obnoxious

Obsolete

Reprehensible

Repugnant

Repulsive

Rancid

Atrocious

Annoying

Awful

Alone

Hateful

Hurtful

Heathen

Hopeless

All words my thoughts spit at me, constantly.

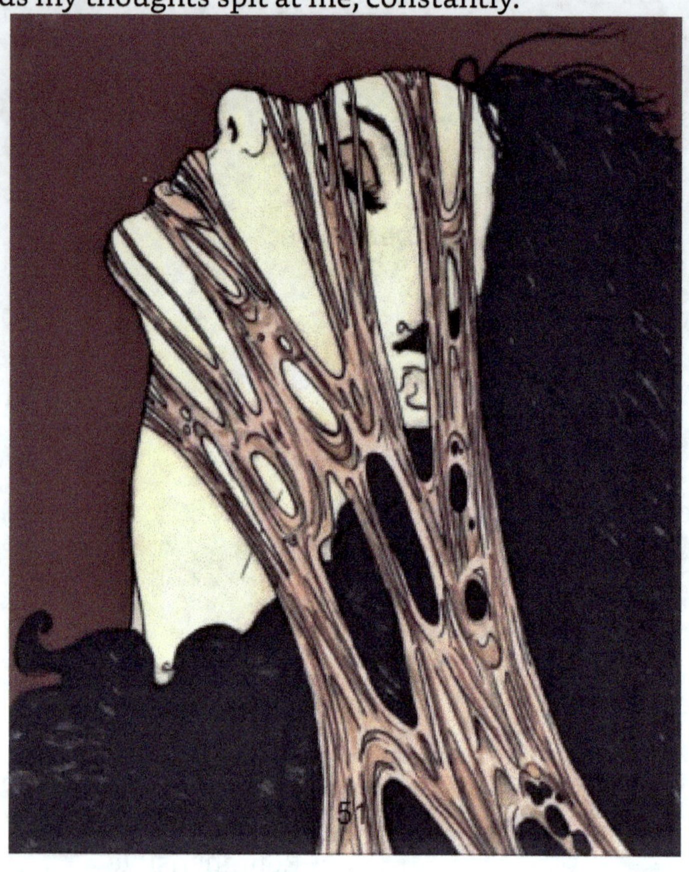

THE MAZE

Is there anybody out there?
Can you hear my cries?
Show yourself, please
Before I fade before my own eyes.

Hello?
I shout as I walk around this maze
My own mind playing tricks
Keeping me here, barely alive.

Another dead end.
I scream into the night.
No not again, I did everything right
Please, no more, I can't take any more.

I take a left, and then a right
Run straight ahead
Two rights then a left
Scale the wall, put there to slow me down

I haven't seen another soul for so long
I'm all alone.
Fighting my own thoughts
Fighting what they conjure up for me to defeat.

Past memories
Mistakes I made
The guilt cripples me
Every
Single
Time.

And then it takes me back to the centre

To try a different route.
I'm tired of doing this by myself
But I've tainted everyone that has tried to help.

I wonder what would happen
If I just decided to stay here?
Would the memories come to find me?
Or could I live in this little haven
For the rest of my days?

There is no getting out
I've tried every conceivable route
Maybe it's time to give in
Admit defeat

Let the thoughts take me, consume me, devour me
Until I'm nothing but a waif
Thrown out with the rubbish
Forgotten about, Ignored, Invisible

Just as I'm about to curl up for the night
Another is dropped in near me
To show me the light

Come, it beckons.
I'll help you leave
We can do this together
I promise I'll never leave.

We take on the maze together
And get much further than before
The exit must be close now
I can feel the hope rising in my chest

Just as we're about to exit
To escape this awful place
I take a look back at the trials and tribulations
The traps that were meant to keep me here, that was my fate.

I say a silent goodbye
And take the step I need
To leave it all behind.
Thanks to my saviour.

FINAL GOODBYE

My life as I knew it has ended
A new chapter has begun
I'm no longer over here stranded
Tied up, burning with the sun.
I'm free, my wings have appeared
To take me away from all I feared.

I'm hurtling forwards, towards my future
Leaving you behind
I watch as you get smaller
The higher up I go
I have no regrets
But it's time for me to go

You're not included in this chapter of my life
And I find that I don't miss you as I thought I might.

Our paths have diverged, where once we thought was one
I've taken the left, and am well on my way to being done.
Your story still has a way to go
Make it bright and lovely to match your soul

Forget about me, my love, for
I was in your life for a scant amount of time
Make memories anew with those left behind

Our lives were never meant to entwine as they did
Which is why my life has splintered off
To give you the remaining time.

To do what you were put on the earth to do
To brighten up the days of everyone you knew
Find the peace in life and yourself

To overcome all the hardships life threw at you, including me.

If we ever meet again, wherever that may be
You'll get a nod and a wave, but that will be all from me

I hope you find the peace you deserve
And the happiness too

I'm sorry for all the torment,
It's been a hard lesson to learn.
That not everyone can love you
In a way that you deserve.

RUNNING.

I am so disorientated.
Wandering the world alone
Wondering if this was what was fated
To be an unknown?

I try to cry out
To make myself heard
But there is no doubt
That this is absurd.

I've walked in the background
Where I wanted to be
Surrounded by people
But none can see me.

I don't like being noticed
Not by anyone.
It makes me uncomfortable
Having their eyes decide whether I'm worthy.

Oi piss off I need to shout.
What I've got here ain't nout.
Scuttle off back into the background I go
Ready to fight friend or foe.

They all start to look the same to me.
I can't differentiate
They've all got faces, mouths, lips, noses, eyes. It's their eyes you
have to watch out for.
They will tell you of danger long before the rest of the body does.
If you don't feel comfortable looking into somebody's eyes, run,
get the hell out from there.

Run, girl, move faster before they catch you.
Run and don't look back.
Keep going until your lungs are fit to burst. And then push on some more.
When you can no longer hear the pursuit
You can take a moment to lean on your knees, get your breath back. Don't stop for too long though. You know they'll be back and they'll want more the second time. Might need to stick a boot in. Scare "em off.

Running, from beasts/memories who knows
We're they even there? Or had your mind conjured up the danger to get you moving to get you someplace else.

And then you hear it. The tell tale sign.
You've run to the railway bridge, and the train is on time.

You boost yourself up onto the wall and time your fall perfectly to end it all.

MISS YOU

I miss you

Why have you gone somewhere I can't follow?
My heart is filled with such sweet sorrow
Did I do something wrong?
I don't know where I belong.

I miss you

Come back, please
I'm begging on my knees
I can't cope without you here.
There is nothing to fear

I miss you

How do I find you again?
Did I miss the omen?
How has the world not stopped turning?
Why am I not learning?

I miss you

You were a part of me
And now you've gone
I really can't see
That we were done.

I miss you

Our story had more to explore
But you walked out the door
Turned your back
What was it that I lack?

I miss you

I'm in agony
I'm struggling to breathe
How can I ever be happy
After watching you leave?

I miss you

I sit in silence
Contemplating where it all went wrong
It was my ignorance
You didn't want to prolong

I miss you

No one will replace you in my life
You were the yin to my yang
I'm sorry for causing such strife
That my confession went off with a bang

I miss you

I never meant to hurt you, to cause any pain
I just wanted to tell the truth, there was no gain
And now I'm sat here alone, where I belong
The memories circled, seeing that I was wrong.

All
gone

FIGHTING

If I could control time I'd go back.
Back before I met you
Back to school
Before then

Before the abuse
Before I was touched
Before I was tainted with this darkness
Before I was broken

I wish I could pretend it never happened
I wish I had been stronger
I wish I had cried for help
I wish it hadn't broke me

I kept it all inside
I kept it hidden
I kept it from everyone
I kept it from you

It fought its way out
Broke down all the walls I had built
To protect myself, you, everyone
It was too much

I told you about what happened
I shared with you details I've never spoken about to anyone
I let myself be vulnerable, again
Opening myself up to be hurt

I treated you badly
I was lashing out
I couldn't live with the images in my head

I had to get out.

There was only one way out, that I could see
But I didn't want to go without saying goodbye first
You meant more to me, than anything else in this world
But, still, I didn't want to be here anymore.

I still don't want to be here
With this stuff inside my head
But I'm trying
I'm fighting so hard

To get back to some sort of 'normal'
To not want to hurt myself every day
To not be 'that' person that ruins everything
To just be.

I'm sorry for being a bitch
I'm sorry for everything
I'm just sorry.

I need to learn to love myself
I need to learn that leaning on others is allowed and encouraged
I need to let go of my past so I can make a better future for myself
I need to forgive me

What happened wasn't my fault
What happened I couldn't have prevented
What happened doesn't have to define me
What happened is not going to defeat me

I'm going to move on
I'm taking steps already
I'm trying to work through everything
I'm trying to get better

I hope my future is bright
I hope I can still be who you thought I was, before I told you
I hope,

I hope,
I hope.

LETTING GO

My past is taking my future
Destroying me from the inside out
The guilt, the helplessness, the pain
Is festering in my blood
Spreading throughout my body
Infiltrating every part, making sure I know
There is no escape.

Keeping me locked into the past
A never ending cycle
Of memories, feelings, thoughts.

Nightmares plague me
I wake in a sweat
The memories fading even as my heart slows
The fear and pain thick in my throat

I cry for the innocence lost
I cry for what could have been
I cry for the girl that didn't know any different
I cry for her.

I've tried to make her future better
I've tried to make her future bright
I've tried to keep her safe

But in my attempts
I've lost myself
I've been consumed
Battling against an invisible foe

I need to let her go
Grieve for the childhood that never was

I need to release her from my mind
Allow her to rise and prosper

Only then can I move on
Only then can I overcome
Only then can I forgive.

Fly high baby girl
I've got it from here.

HUMAN

Watching you get taken away
And knowing there was nothing
I could do to change it
Absolutely broke me

You were an innocent
And I let you down
I'm so sorry
That I let them take you.

You weren't mine to fight for
You weren't mine to save
But if I had had the power, the means
I would have.

I would have sacrificed myself for you
I should have done more
To keep you with your siblings
To keep you in the family.

Your siblings were taken a few months before you
I was helpless then too

I hope you all know that we love you
I hope you all know that we think of you constantly
I hope you all know that life hasn't been the same since you were
taken

I'm sorry.

I hope your life has been good
That you have known love
I hope that you are happy
That you have everything you need

If in the future you want to find us
Please do
Reach out, and we will embrace you
We've missed so much

Please don't hate us
We had no say in what happened
Your mother fucked us over
Made us out to be the monsters

We've only ever tried to help
We've only ever tried to support
We've only ever tried to do the right thing
If only we had tried harder.

Forgive us.
We are only human.

UNWANTED LOVE

My love for you burns brighter than the sun
Blinding you so you can't see
You feel the warmth caress your skin
But turn your back so as not to acknowledge it

My love for you is unwanted
Categorised as a charade
It's not something you're willing to accept
For the fear of falling under

Being burnt, enflamed, consumed by my feelings
Is not something you want to endure
But I have no choice in the matter
I gave myself willingly to the sun

Letting it spread its love all over my skin
Embraced it, let it soak in
That love has sustained me for so long
Having it rejected knocked me back

Now the love is bubbling, changing
I need it to change to self love
Self care, self worth.
The love for you is still there, under it all, directing it, trying to
help it go where it needs.

Even though you aren't here
Even though you rejected me
You are still my best friend
You are still my favourite person

You mean more to me than anything
You mean absolutely everything

Being without you is torture
Being without you is death.

I REALLY WANT TO SEE YOU

I really want to see you
To feel you in my arms
To see the smile on your face
Would make me truly calm

I really want to talk to you
To catch up with the news
To simply be in your company
Would be genuinely heavenly

I'd pull you close
And hold you near
Squeeze you into my embrace
Quieting my fears

I'd wipe my tears behind your back
Soaking in the feeling
Appreciating the moment
For what it is.

But I fear this will never happen
As we have become estranged
Our friendship has become misshapen
I wish it was unchanged.

This punishment is torture
Something I bought on myself
You were collateral damage
To my mental health

I'm sorry for everything I've done
For causing you so much hurt
I hope one day we can meet

And lay this all to rest

I really want to see you
To feel you in my arms.
Just to share a room with you
Would be a truly nice start.

A CONVERSATION

Oh my God
What happened to me?
Why didn't I do more?
Couldn't you protect me?

I'm sorry, to tell you
You were abused
I wasn't old enough to help
It happened to me too.

How do I get past this?
The memories are horrid
The feel of his hands
Makes my skin crawl

I know baby
I was there too
I don't know how it happened
But I'm going to get us through.

I tried to make myself small
To not bring attention to myself
It didn't make a bit of difference
He still came for me.

Again, I'm sorry baby
I'm doing what I can
To get us answers
To try to understand

Why did this happen?
Did I do something wrong?
It's all my fault

I never called a halt

This isn't your fault
Stop thinking like that
He groomed and abused you
You didn't stand a chance

I want to hide
I want to cry
I want to scream
Why would you do this?

Cry and scream
Let it out
I can't give you the answers you seek
We weren't weak
It was a case of opportunity
We were there
He got to work his evil on us
But we need to work past this
To move on
Let it all out, baby
I'll be strong for both of us.

We're not going to let you beat us
We're not going to let you taint us anymore
We're going to move past this
We're going to come out stronger.

PUNISHER - A DRABBLE

I give in
I can't fight anymore
Take me down the road to hell
I'll follow you anywhere

As I stand by your side
I feel your possessiveness
It surrounds me like a storm
It's better than feeling nothing

I watch as you decide others fates
Preside over your domain
You've made me your understudy
I'm meant to replace you when you've gone

I'm numb to everything that's going on
As I watch, a paedophile burns at your hand
I feel a flicker of something ignite
I can do this, I can make them suffer

I become enthralled
Asking question after question
All the people that come through here
Are murderers, child abusers, burglars, money launderers.

The scum of the earth
And we get to deliver them to evil
Send them on their way with the flames licking at their skin
I smile as I watch one go, the terror in his eyes satisfying.

We do to them what they do to their victims
Play their life in front of them
Make sure they know there here to burn for their sins for all

eternity
Once they realise their fate, and their eyes widen in fear

We step forward
And send them to their end
The screams and begging the last thing we hear
As the flames take their next victim.

And as the next one drops onto the platform
You usher me forward
You're offering this one to me
I smile and move forward ready to do what is needed

Except I recognise this piece of filth
As the man that broke me
I freeze in place for a moment
The memories taking me back

I watch as his film plays
And see myself through his eyes
The horrible things he did to me
When I was a child

I step forward and shout his name
This isn't normal protocol
But I need him to know
I'm the one that's going to finish him

His eyes meet mine across the arena
I see a moment of recognition
And then the fear is his eyes
The same that had been in mine all those years ago

I make the gesture to open the floor beneath him
As it begins to tremble, to do as I bequeathed
He begs me to let him go
To offer him salvation

The flames reflect off my eyes

As I watch him burn
I've never felt an emotion quite like this
Peace, tranquility and vengeance.

As the floor begins to close
It's job accomplished
I turn to the one that brought me here
And nod in acceptance of their terms.
I will preside over the underworld
Punishing the guilty that got away with their crimes
And I will enjoy every moment
Until it becomes my time.

LOVE/HATE

How much do you hate me?
As much as I love you?
They say there's a thin line between the two
It gets blurred and crossed so many times.

Which is the stronger emotion?
Love or hate?
One can make life beautiful
The other is another form of hell.

I've hated myself pretty much all my life
And loved a scant few
But true, breathtaking love?
That was reserved just for you.

It could have wonderful
It could have been great
But you had already found your forever mate

I've suffered in silence
Basking in the glow
Of a love that was never mine
Watching as you grow.

You went from one to two
Then three and four
And still I kept quiet
As I wasn't meritorious

You'd have never accepted the love I had to offer
So I kept it to myself
I never made a proffer
I wanted to save myself, as selfish as that sounds

I don't believe I deserve such a life
One that is shared and not full of strife
So I sabotaged the only thing that's ever meant anything to me
So I couldn't bring you down with me.

So now I sit, all alone
Exactly as I deserve
Imagining a life where I told you
Just exactly how much you're loved

I hope that you are happy
I hope you're life is full
I hope that my sacrifice was worth it
As I sit here in the cull.

Cast off like a ship
That's never to return
Cursed by the one that found it
Forever to be alone.

FIND A WAY

Everyone says 'life is short'
That you should appreciate every moment
And whilst I don't disagree
I believe that there comes a point in a person's life
Where they have endured enough heartache and disappointment
and despair
That they feel life isn't worth living anymore.

When that threshold is reached
They only see one way out
And there's nothing anyone can say to help
To change their mind
If they've already gotten to this point
You can guarantee that they've already
Troubleshooted, tried to work through
Whatever it is that tipped them over the edge.

Already reached out to friends and family
Tried to get the help they need from 'professionals'
Doctors, nurses, psychologists, the supposed 'mental health team'
And have felt fobbed off by every single one.
There are only so many pills, talking therapies, meditations that a
person can try
Before they reach the end of their tether.

And I'm not saying that ending your life is the right way to go
But I can understand that feeling
I've been there myself
Where the memories, and life was just too difficult to cope with.
Wanting to get away, to not have to deal with it all.

I'm not going to say

'There's light at the end of the tunnel'
'It's not going to be this bad forever'
'A problem shared is a problem halved'

But what I am going to say is this
YOU ARE WORTH IT
YOU CAN DEFEAT THIS
No problem is that big, that you can't overcome it.
KEEP TRYING
KEEP FORGING FORWARD

Someone will be glad that you're still here
Someone will need you
Someone loves you
Even if you don't know who that person is.
They will make themselves known to you, when the time is right.

If in doubt, please reach out.
My inbox is always open.
Don't take that final step, without being absolutely sure that your
life isn't worth anything.
That no one will grieve for you
That you won't be missed.
That you won't break someone's heart when they hear the news.

Suicide is not the end of your story
There's still so much to go
I'm sorry you've felt you can't go on
That suicide has even crossed your mind.
Find a way to overcome
Find a way to get through the day
Just FIND A WAY

UNREQUITED LOVE

I hope you're doing fine
I'd put my life on the line
We were going to be forever
Until you said never

We'd known each other since school
Neither of us was a fool
We were as thick as thieves
My whole life was a dream

You met another
Made them your lover
I was cast off, set adrift
I couldn't see what was amiss

I stayed in the background
There were no cracks to be found
I wilted away
Watching you sway
On you're wedding day
I was your maid of honour
I never meant to dishonour

I hope you're doing fine
I'd put my life on the line
We were going to be forever
Until you said never

Our lives did diverge
We became estranged
You're life blossomed
Whilst mine had tanked

We reconnected after a few years
I shared all of my fears
You helped me through some bad stuff
It had been enough

But then my feelings got in the way
I didn't want to stay
I did my best to hide them
To refrain from being condemned

But one night
I got myself in a plight
I turned to you, and told you
That you had always had my heart

I hope you're doing fine
I'd put my life on the line
We were going to be forever
Until you said never

This confession wasn't well received
I sank down to my knees
You looked at me in disgust
And left me there, aghast

My heart broke into a million pieces
Never to be rebuilt
Our relationship was over
I was no longer a pushover

There's been no contact
For over a month
I've been working on myself
Since we've been separated
Trying to fix my heart
Wondering how you are

I hope you're doing fine

I'd put my life on the line
We were going to be forever
Until you said never

I'm on my way to being better
I've written you a letter
I hope you can read it
Can forgive me at some point

I never meant to cause an issue
I never meant to let you know
I never meant for any of this
I really hope you can forgive me

I hope you have been well
I hope you never fell
I hope you have the support you need
That you can continue to believe
That you are the shining star
That I know you are

I hope you're doing fine
I'd put my life on the line
We were going to be forever
Until you said never.

I'M GOING TO WIN

I sit with my eyes closed
Blocking out the light
Trying to center myself
So I'm ready to face the night

The nights are always worst
When my demons come to play
When my memories come back to haunt me
It's all so fucking daunting.

I get as peaceful as I can
Before settling down to sleep
But I know my dreams will become nightmares
Before the night is out.

It always starts the same
Me, as a child, sitting being good
And then a shadow passes over me
And I feel the flood

The flood of endorphins
As I get told off
For something that wasn't my fault
Then when you see me again, I'm older

And I'm doing to others what you did to me
Doing things that are forbidden and disgusting
I'm not in control of my hands
I try to withstand

I wake screaming
My hands around my throat
My eyes are streaming

I'm barely keeping afloat

Just the thought of doing that
Makes me physically sick
I want to buy a bat
To beat myself with

I imagine turning this on you
Beating you black and blue
Taking back what you took from me
My childhood, my innocence

But then I'd be as bad as you
So I turn it all on myself
Hold myself to higher standards
Never letting up

Punishing myself for every little thing
That may be seen as a slight
Berating myself viciously
For all of my life

I need to stop hating on myself
Be kinder to the younger me
Let her grow wings and go free
Live a happy life, my dear, I've got it from here.

Now to my abuser
I'll never be like you
No matter how much you try to manipulate
To try to make me a conspirator

I'm stronger than you think
I'm no longer weak
You can't control me anymore
I will no longer endure

You thought that you had broken me
Made me into what you wanted

But I came back fighting
I resisted you're mind games

I'm now in my thirties
And my life isn't what I thought it would be
But I'm still here, confronting my fears
You will not defeat me, let me make that clear

You are a lying, sick, pathetic excuse of a man
And I'm taking back my life, you're no longer going to cause me strife.
I cast you out of my story
So I can enjoy the glory.

I need to take control of my future
Make it what I deserve
I need to be kind and nurture
And not be adverse

To accepting help
From friends and family
Move on from the horror of what you did
To no longer let you interfere even though you're not even here

I'M DONE!

I'm so broken
There's nothing left to see
I've been broken for a while
I'm beginning to realize that there's no point.

No point in trying to heal
No point in reaching out
No point in my existence
No point in any of it.

I should just stop breathing, eating, surviving.
As that's all I can do.
Survive until the next battle looms
Survive until I've destroyed it all.

I'm done with being strong
I'm done with the fight
I'm done trying to be what others need
I'm done being me.

MY CHOICE

Why can't you accept my choice?
Listen to the tone of my voice
I'm sick of being sad.
Is it really so bad?

I don't want to be here anymore
I don't want to endure
I'm done
I'm overcome

The thoughts, the memories, the feelings
My emotions have been reeling
I can't live with them on replay
I'll do it someday.

I'm sorry if this makes you sad
But It's driving me mad
I can't keep doing this
I'm not doing this to take the piss
Nothings amiss

Thank you for everything you've done
Don't blame yourself, I was overthrown
Mourn me if you must, love
But move on, live your life, you're not done.

I'll wait for you on the other side
Where we can reconcile
I wanted to confide
I never meant to be hostile.

Goodbye my friend
I never meant to condescend

Thank you for trying
There's no use my denying

I fought for as long as I could
But I was misunderstood
I'm at peace now
I hope you don't think I'm a cow.

My peace of mind having you accept this decision
Would do me the world of good
I can go off then, meet my maker
On my terms, with your blessing.